DIGITAL PLANET

HOW DOES
THE INTERNET WORK?

by Nikole Brooks Bethea

Ideas for Parents and Teachers

Pogo Books let children practice reading informational text while introducing them to nonfiction features such as headings, labels, sidebars, maps, and diagrams, as well as a table of contents, glossary, and index.

Carefully leveled text with a strong photo match offers early fluent readers the support they need to succeed.

Before Reading

- "Walk" through the book and point out the various nonfiction features. Ask the student what purpose each feature serves.
- Look at the glossary together. Read and discuss the words.

Read the Book

- Have the child read the book independently.
- Invite him or her to list questions that arise from reading.

After Reading

- Discuss the child's questions. Talk about how he or she might find answers to those questions.
- Prompt the child to think more. Ask: What do you use the internet for? Have you ever thought about how it works?

Pogo Books are published by Jump!
5357 Penn Avenue South
Minneapolis, MN 55419
www.jumplibrary.com

Library of Congress Cataloging-in-Publication Data

Names: Bethea, Nikole Brooks, author.
Title: How does the internet work? / by Nikole Brooks Bethea.
Description: Pogo Books | Minneapolis, MN: Jump!, Inc., [2020] | Series: Digital planet
Audience: Ages 7-10. | Includes index.
Identifiers: LCCN 2018059560 (print)
LCCN 2019002407 (ebook)
ISBN 9781641288897 (ebook)
ISBN 9781641288873 (hardcover: alk. paper)
ISBN 9781641288880 (pbk.)
Subjects: LCSH: Internet–Juvenile literature. Computer literacy–Juvenile literature.
Classification: LCC TK5105.875.I57 (ebook)
LCC TK5105.875.I57 B4845 2020 (print)
DDC 004.67/8–dc23
LC record available at https://lccn.loc.gov/2018059560

Editor: Susanne Bushman
Designer: Michelle Sonnek
Content Consultant: Sarah McRoberts, Human-Computer Interaction Researcher

Photo Credits: Konstantin Faraktinov/Shutterstock, cover (top); Ratana21/Shutterstock, cover (bottom); shapecharge/iStock, 1 (girl); Avector/Shutterstock, 1 (tablet background); Kidsada Manchinda/Shutterstock, 3 (computer); hardqor4ik/Shutterstock, 3 (screen); Oleksiy Maksymenko/SuperStock, 4; Sjoerd van der Wal/iStock, 5; patat/Shutterstock, 6-7; Kaspars Grinvalds/Shutterstock, 6-7 (web page); Nixx Photography/Shutterstock, 8-9; Shutterstock, 10-11 (background); Welshea Photography/Shutterstock, 10-11 (screen); blue_iq/iStock, 10-11 (modem); sirikorn thamniyom/Shutterstock, 12 (girl); Alexey Boldin/Shutterstock, 12 (screen); Federico Rostagno/Shutterstock, 13; Castleski/Shutterstock, 14-15; David MG/Shutterstock, 16-17; Denis Dryashkin/Shutterstock, 18; Prostock-studio/Shutterstock, 19 (background); Ryzhi/Shutterstock, 19 (screen); JPL/NASA, 20-21; IB Photography/Shutterstock, 23.

Printed in the United States of America at Corporate Graphics in North Mankato, Minnesota.

TABLE OF CONTENTS

CHAPTER 1

HOW THE INTERNET WORKS

Most cars go to the shop if they break down. But not Teslas! **Software** in these cars can be fixed over the internet!

Tesla

How? These cars connect to the internet through **Wi-Fi**.

But what is the internet? It is a **network** of many devices. We use the **World Wide Web** to browse the internet. How? We use **browsers**. Google Chrome is one. Safari is another. Web pages show us text, videos, and photos.

web page

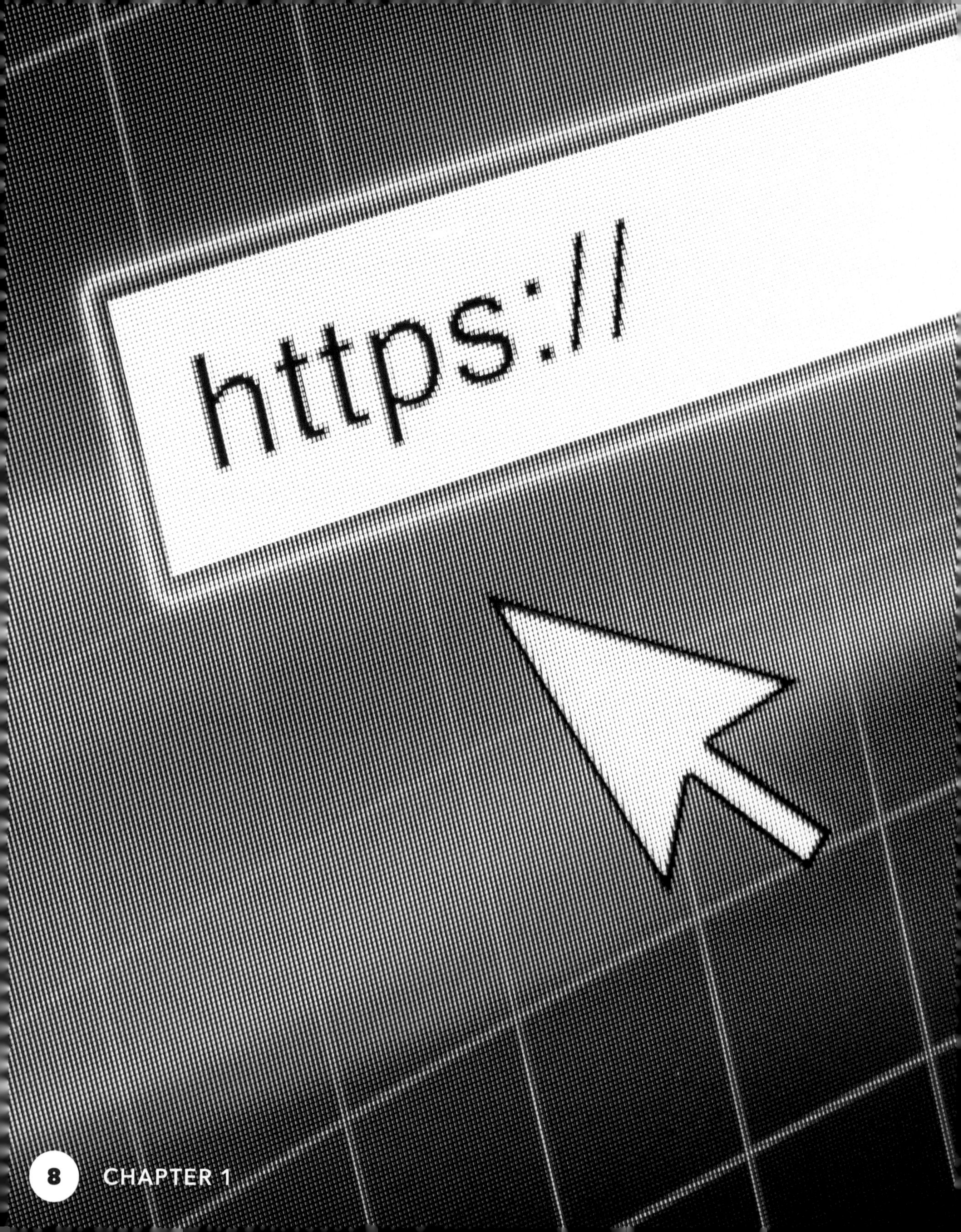
https://

Browsers use **HTTPS**. This is a set of rules. The rules tell devices how to share **data**.

Many web addresses start with https://. This tells the device to look for a file shared on the internet.

Web pages are broken into small **packets**. The packets move along paths on the internet. A **modem** translates the data for your computer. A **router** directs the data to your device. Your device pieces the packets back together. You see what you were looking for!

modem

Cute Corgi   New Tab

https://www.dogs.com

How does a web page get from the internet to your device? Take a look!

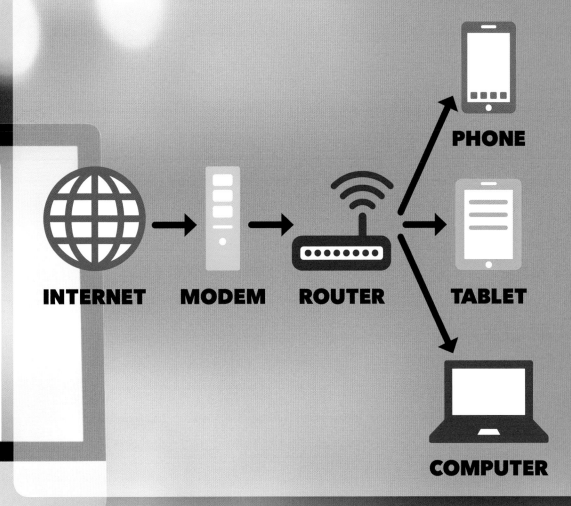

INTERNET   MODEM   ROUTER

PHONE

TABLET

COMPUTER

CHAPTER 2

USING THE INTERNET

Many of us use the internet to connect with each other. Friends and family are just clicks away. We video chat. We email. We send instant messages. Many of us use social media.

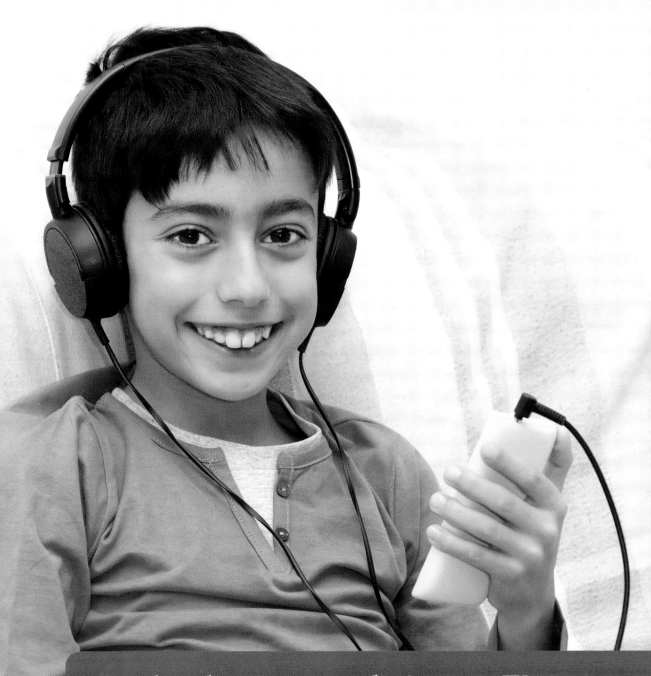

We also play games on the internet. We can listen to music. **Streaming** movies is fun, too! Do you download ebooks?

What is the score of the game? Where is Spain? Will it be sunny today? You can type in any question! **Search engines** like Google can answer them all!

ONLINEPIZZA

2x1

- AMERICAN
- CHEESE SPECIAL
- X-LARGE SPECIAL
- VEGGIE PIZZA
- GLUTEN FREE
- CHIPS
- DRINKS

ORDER NOW!

You can also find businesses. Most have web pages. You can buy everything from pizza to books to concert tickets online!

CHAPTER 3

THE INTERNET'S FUTURE

Most devices connect with a wireless router. It sends out radio waves. Devices pick them up. They connect.

wireless
router

That could change! What's next? A special LED light bulb could act as a router. It does not send radio waves. It sends visible light waves instead. How? It flickers at high speed. Devices can detect the flickers.

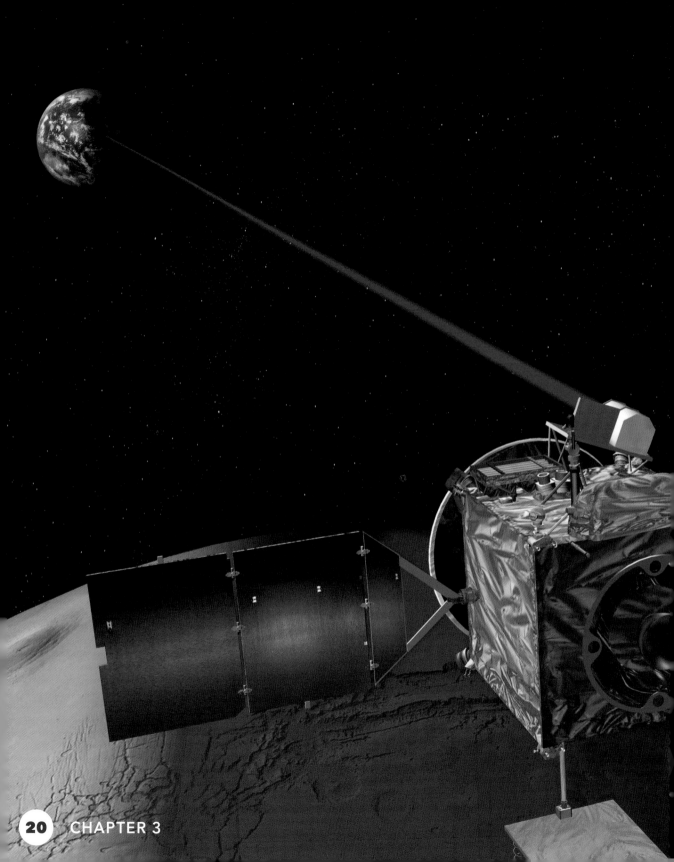

Lasers could be next. **NASA** wants to turn data into laser light. Why? They could send data from space to Earth.

We can do many things on the internet! What do you do online?

ACTIVITIES & TOOLS

DESIGN A WEB PAGE

If you had a business, what would it sell? What would the website look like? Make your own business website!

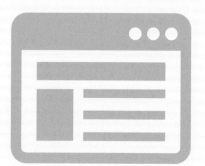

What You Need:

- paper
- pencil
- crayons, markers, or colored pencils

❶ Create a name for your business. Does it have a logo? Draw one!

❷ Draft a design for your web page. What will it look like? What colors would you like it to be? Where will the name and logo be?

❸ Think about each part of the web page. What happens when you click there?

❹ What different sections does your web page need? Where will visitors see products, prices, and contact information? Draw how you want it to look.

❺ Color the design.

browsers: Applications used to access websites on the internet, such as Internet Explorer, Mozilla Firefox, Google Chrome, and Safari.

cloud: A network of remote servers that store data instead of using local hard drive storage.

data: Information collected in a place so something can be done with it.

HTTPS: Short for hypertext transfer protocol secure; the set of rules used to connect websites over the internet.

modem: A device that converts signals from one type of network to be compatible with another.

NASA: Short for National Aeronautics and Space Administration; the government agency responsible for space exploration and research.

network: A group of connected computer systems.

packets: Small units of data that have been broken down to travel along a network.

router: A device that guides data packets along routes over an electronic communications network.

search engines: Computer programs that search the World Wide Web for information.

servers: Computers that store files that can be accessed through the internet.

software: Computer programs that control the workings of a device or piece of equipment and direct it to do specific tasks.

streaming: Digitally transferring in a single, continuous flow.

supercomputers: Very powerful computers that can compute quickly and are often used by scientists, businesses, and the military.

Wi-Fi: A wireless signal that allows computers and other devices to connect to the internet wherever a signal is available.

World Wide Web: The system of websites connected on the internet.

INDEX

TO LEARN MORE

Finding more information is as easy as 1, 2, 3.

1 Go to www.factsurfer.com

2 Enter "howdoestheinternetwork?" into the search box.

3 Choose your book to see a list of websites.

FACT SURFER